Dealing With

OUR
NEW BABY

by Jane Lacey
Illustrated by Venitia Dean

W
FRANKLIN WATTS
LONDON • SYDNEY

Franklin Watts
First published in Great Britain in 2017 by The Watts Publishing Group

Copyright © The Watts Publishing Group, 2017
The text in this book was originally published in the series 'How can I deal with'

Credits
Series Editor: Sarah Peutrill
Series Design: Collaborate

Every attempt has been made to clear copyright. Should there be any
inadvertent omission please apply to the publisher for rectification.

ISBN 978 1 4451 5793 1

Printed in China

Franklin Watts
An imprint of
Hachette Children's Group
Part of The Watts Publishing Group
Carmelite House
50 Victoria Embankment
London EC4Y 0DZ

An Hachette UK Company
www.hachette.co.uk

www.franklinwatts.co.uk

FSC
www.fsc.org

MIX
Paper from
responsible sources
FSC® C104740

Contents

I DON'T WANT A NEW BABY!

Ellie's mum and dad are happy because they are expecting a baby. Ellie's little sister Jenny is excited, but Ellie isn't. She doesn't want a new baby in the family.

Jenny is Ellie's little sister

Our new baby is going to have my bedroom. I'm going to share my big sister Ellie's bedroom. I'm happy but Ellie is grumpy about the baby and she's really grumpy with me!

Jenny

Ellie's story

When Mum and Dad told Jenny and me and about the new baby, Jenny jumped up and down and said, "We're having a new baby!" over and over again. I pretended to be pleased, but I'm not really. I've got to share my bedroom with Jenny. She can be a real pest! Mum and Dad, Jenny and me all play tennis together. We won't be able to with a new baby. Babies are a nuisance! They cry and have smelly nappies. I don't think I'll love a new baby.

Ellie

What can Ellie do?

She doesn't have to pretend to be pleased. She can:

★ tell her mum and dad she doesn't think she'll love the new baby
★ say she doesn't want things to change
★ say she wishes she didn't have to share a room with Jenny.

What Ellie did

Mum and Dad were glad I talked to them. I think they knew how I felt already! They said it can take time to get used to a new baby, but changes can be exciting. Jenny and I are helping to decorate our room and the baby's room. We're getting bunk beds. I'm having the top bunk!

EXPECTING A BABY

A baby grows in its mother's womb. It grows very slowly, so there is plenty of time to get ready. As the baby grows, the mother's tummy gets bigger and bigger. After about five months, you can feel the baby move and kick if you put your hand gently on the mother's bump. For the first few months, a mother sometimes feels sick. As her tummy gets bigger, she can feel uncomfortable and tired. After nine months, the baby is ready to be born.

I'M WORRIED THAT MUM AND THE BABY WON'T BE ALL RIGHT

Liam's mum is expecting a baby. His dad is looking after her extra carefully and keeps asking her if she's all right. Now Liam's worried she won't be all right.

Jayden

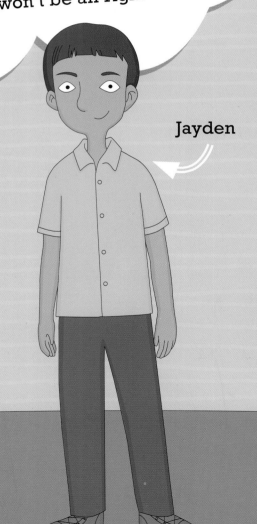

Jayden is Liam's friend

Liam keeps asking me about when my baby sister was born. I don't know - she was just born! She was OK and Mum was OK. Why shouldn't they be? I wish he wouldn't go on about it.

Mum's having a baby. I hope it's a boy, but it might be a girl. Jayden's baby sister is OK I suppose.

Dad keeps fussing over Mum as if something bad might happen. Is something bad going to happen? How can I tell?

When I ask Jayden about his mum having a baby, he says he can't remember. Then he says it'll be fine and don't worry!

But I am worried. I want Mum and the baby to be all right.

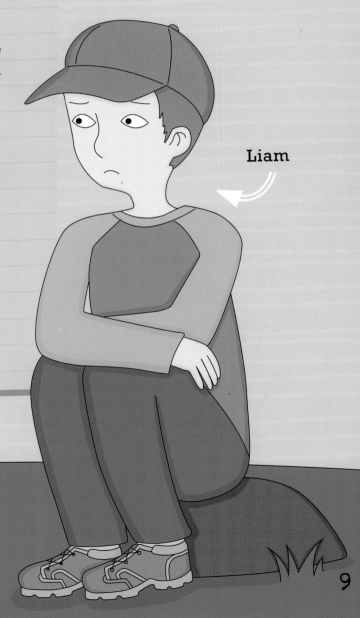

Liam

9

what can Liam do?

Liam is worried because he doesn't know why Dad is fussing over Mum. He can:

★ talk to his dad
★ ask him why he seems to be worried
★ say now he's feeling worried, too.

what Liam did

I talked to Dad. He said I was born early. I had to stay in hospital for weeks. He was worried it might happen again.

But now we are both worrying less. Mum is very well and so is the baby. I've seen the scan of our baby. It looks like a frog!

GETTING READY FOR THE BABY

Fran was excited about having a new baby brother or sister.

First we decorated the baby's room. Then we went shopping.

We bought so much stuff, just for one tiny baby!

Mum got bigger and bigger until one day she said, "The baby's coming!"

Dad took Mum to hospital. Nan looked after me. I made a card and wrapped a teddy for the baby.

Dad phoned and said, "It's a girl!" I was one of the first people to see her. She pulled a funny face at me but I think she likes me.

THE NEW BABY IS BORING!

Frankie was looking forward to having a baby brother to play with. But baby Charlie is too little to play. Frankie thinks he's boring.

Baby Charlie only sleeps, eats, cries and has smelly nappies. Sometimes he just does nothing. Mum and Dad expect me to play with him, but there's no point. I'll wait until he's old enough.

Frankie's story

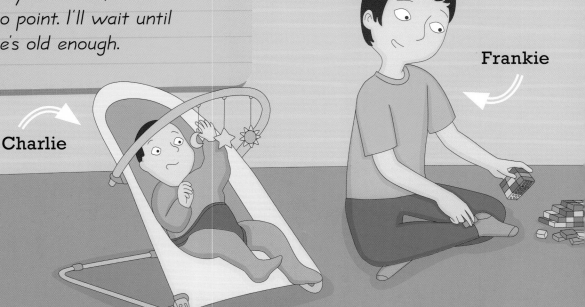

Charlie

Frankie

What can Frankie do?

There are lots of things Frankie can do for baby Charlie. He can:

★ help dress, bath and burp him
★ hold him carefully when he's sitting down
★ help push his buggy when they go out for a walk
★ talk to him, tell him stories and sing to him.

Baby Charlie will soon get to know him. Frankie might be the first person he smiles at. Soon Frankie will be able to make baby Charlie laugh.

It won't be long before they are good friends.

13

I'M JEALOUS OF THE NEW BABY

Mia knows she should love her baby sister, but she feels jealous of all the attention the baby gets. Mia wishes she had Mum and Dad to herself again.

Kirsty is Mia's friend

When I went to Mia's house to see the new baby, Mia kept trying to pull me away.

She said, "Play with me!" I said, "I want to play with baby Lola." Now Mia says I'm not her friend any more!

Kirsty

Mia

Mia's Story

Everyone comes round and makes a fuss of Lola. They don't take any notice of me.

I feel really left out.

I had Mum and Dad all to myself before baby Lola was born. Now I've got to share them. And it's not even fair shares. Lola gets loads of attention. I only get a teeny-weeny little bit.

I think Mum and Dad love baby Lola more than me. I think everyone loves her more than me! Sometimes I wish she had never been born.

What can Mia do?

Lots of children feel jealous of a new baby. She can:

★ tell her mum and dad she feels left out
★ say she thinks they love the baby more than her
★ say she felt happier before.

What Mia did

Mia told her mum and dad she thinks they love the baby more than her. Mum and Dad said they love me just as much as ever. Now they love Lola, too.

There's plenty of love to go round. So when Lola's asleep, Mum or Dad have a special time with me. I let Kirsty play with Lola, as long as she spends lots of time with me, too!

MY BABY BROTHER IS A NUISANCE!

Jade's baby brother Barney cries at night and wakes her up. Mum and Dad are tired. Her big sister Anna helps look after the baby. Jade thinks Barney's a nuisance.

Anna is Jade's big sister

Anna

Jade is cross all the time. She is cross with baby Barney, cross with Mum and Dad and cross with me. I can't play with her much because I'm busy helping Mum look after baby Barney.

Jade's story

Everyone says how sweet baby Barney is.

I suppose he is, sometimes, but mostly he's a nuisance! He cries all night and keeps everyone awake. Mum and Dad are always tired.

If he gives a little whimper, Anna rushes to look after him - even if we're in the middle of a game.

Now he's crawling, he knocks over my toys and puts them in his mouth.

It takes ages to dress him and put him in his buggy every time we go out.

What can Jade do?

Babies need lots of care and attention. They take up a lot of time. She can:

★ tell her big sister she's cross because she thinks baby Barney is a nuisance

★ find ways she can help out with Barney and join in.

what Jade did

I talked to Anna. She said she'd play with me more. Now I'm helping with Barney. I read him books and he tries to eat them. I put on his hat and he pulls it off.

I feed him and he blows his food at me. When I laugh at him, he giggles, too!

I WANT TO HELP!

When baby Alex was born, Gemma wanted to look after him.

Gemma's Mum's Story

One day, baby Alex was crying in his bedroom and he suddenly stopped. I ran upstairs to find out why. Gemma had picked him up out of his cot.

I was really cross with her. She could have dropped him! She cried and said she was only trying to help.

I said, "I know you love Alex and want to help, but you are too young to do it all by yourself. You can help me and we'll look after Alex together."

WATCHING A BABY GROW

New babies can't do anything for themselves. They cry to get attention. Crying can mean, "I'm hungry! I've got a dirty nappy! I'm bored! I'm tired!" Sometimes it can mean, "Help, I've got a pain!"

Babies soon begin to smile. They get stronger and can sit up and hold things. You can read to them, play with them and make them giggle. At six months, some babies begin to crawl. At twelve months, they may learn to walk. You can hold their hands to help them.

Babies can be lots of fun, but always ask an adult to help you play with a baby.

MY LITTLE SISTER ALWAYS GETS HER OWN WAY!

Jesse's little sister Hetty has just learned to walk. She can say a few words. Jesse thinks his mum and dad expect him to give in to her.

Aiden is Jesse's friend

Jesse always wants to come round and play at my house. He says he wants to get away from his baby sister. That's all right with me. Hetty spoils all our games!

Aiden

22

Jesse's story

When baby Hetty was tiny, she was really sweet. I was the first person she smiled at!

She was funny when she fed herself. Everything got covered in food!

Now she can toddle and say a few words, she gets away with everything!

I always have to do what Hetty wants. Mum and Dad say, "Give it to her, Jesse! Play with her, Jesse! She's only little."

If she cries they say, "What have you done, Jesse?" when I haven't even done anything! I don't think she's sweet any more!

Jesse

Santa's Bear

23

What can Jesse do?

It can be hard to love a baby brother or sister all the time. Jesse can:

★ tell his mum and dad he wants to love Hetty
★ say he doesn't think it's fair he is expected to give in to her
★ say he is finding it hard to love her all the time.

What Jesse did

I told Mum and Dad. They said Hetty is old enough to understand "no". When they say "no", she doesn't like it and makes a fuss. Mum distracts her and she quickly forgets it. Aiden comes round to my house again now that Hetty doesn't always get her own way.

24

WILL MY STEPDAD STILL LOVE ME?

Kayo's mum and stepdad are having a baby together. Her friend Padma is worried about her.

Padma

Padma is Kayo's friend

Kayo's been sad since she heard about the new baby. I thought she'd be happy.

She doesn't want to talk about it. I wish I knew why the new baby is making her sad.

Kayo's Story

My mum and dad are divorced. I live with Mum and my stepdad. I don't see my own dad very often, but I get on really well with my stepdad, Phil.

Phil hasn't got any other children, only me.

He says I'm his little girl.

I know my mum will always love me.

But Phil's so happy he and Mum are having a baby, I'm afraid he won't love me when he's got a baby of his own.

What can Kayo do?

No one can help Kayo unless she tells them why she's sad. She can:

* ★ tell her friend Padma she thinks Phil won't love her when the baby arrives
* ★ tell her mum
* ★ tell Phil.

what Kayo did

I told Padma and she said Phil wouldn't stop loving me. I told Mum and she said the same. Phil gave me a hug and he said the same! He said I would be a very special big sister. Now I'm looking forward to the new baby and I'm not sad any more.

OUR NEW BABY

When Bonnie and Grace first heard their mum was going to have a new baby, they didn't know what to think.

Bonnie:

Mum and Dad were really excited about having a new baby. Grace and I weren't so sure!

Grace:

Babies need lots of looking after and they can't do much. I thought a new baby would spoil our fun.

Bonnie:

Mum and Dad just expected us to be pleased, so at first we pretended to be happy about our new baby brother or sister.

Grace:

But we couldn't fool Mum and Dad. They wanted to know what was going on.

Bonnie:
I told them - I think having a baby will change everything. I like things just as they are. I said a baby will stop us all doing things together like going swimming or going out for pizza.

Grace: Mum told us that the baby will change lots of things, but they can be good changes.

Bonnie: Dad said he'd make sure we still did the things we enjoy.

Grace: Mum said it wouldn't be long before the baby could join in, too.

Bonnie: When baby Pete was born I thought he was really sweet.

Grace: I helped bath and dress him. I thought he was noisy and smelly! But I liked the way he held onto my finger and pulled funny faces at me.

Bonnie: Now baby Pete is learning to walk. We make him laugh and he can nearly say our names. Now we can't imagine not having him around.

GLOSSARY

Attention
You are given attention when other people take notice of you and spend time with you.

Born
A baby is born when it is ready to leave its mother's womb and live separately from her.

Fair
A rule or a decision is fair when it is good for everyone involved.

Jealous
You feel jealous when you think someone else is getting more love and attention than you and that makes you unhappy.

Nuisance
Someone is a nuisance when they stop you doing what you want to do, or they are annoying.

Pretend
You pretend when you make other people believe something is true when it isn't really.

Scan
A photograph taken of an unborn baby in its mother's womb.

Share
You share when you tell or give things to other people and you don't keep things to yourself.

Womb
The part of a mother's body where a baby grows until it is ready to be born.

Worry
You worry when you feel toubled about something.

Further Information

For children

www.childline.org.uk
Tel: 0800 1111
Childline is a free helpline for children in the UK. You can talk to someone about any problem and they will help you to sort it out.

www.kidshealth.org
Confused, sad, mad, glad? Check out the 'Feelings' section to learn about these emotions and others – and how to deal with them.

For readers in Australia and New Zealand

www.cyh.com
Loads of online information about all sorts of issues.

www.kidshelp.com.au
Tel: 1800 55 1800
Kidshelp is the free helpline for children in Australia. You can talk to someone about any problem.

www.kidsline.org.nz
A helpline run by specially trained young volunteers to help kids and teens deal with troubling issues and problems.

For parents

www.parentlineplus.org.uk
Helpline for parents:
0808 800 2222
ParentLine Plus offers advice, guidance and support for parents who are concerned about their children.

www.bbc.co.uk/parenting/
having_a_baby/

Note to parents and teachers: Every effort has been made by the Publishers to ensure these websites are suitable for children, that they are of the highest educational value and that they contain no inappropriate or offensive material. However, because of the nature of the Internet, it is impossible to guarantee that the contents of these sites will not be altered. We strongly advise that Internet access is supervised by a responsible adult.

INDEX

Notes for parents, carers and teachers

Many children will be happy and excited about the arrival of a new baby. Others will feel jealous and resent the changes that a new baby brings. There are many ways parents, carers and teachers can help children to deal with a new baby.

- Reassuring your child that they are still very special and that there is enough love to go round for everyone helps them not to feel threatened by a new baby.
- Encouraging your child to help with washing, dressing and playing with the new baby will help them to feel involved and not left out.
- It helps to have special time alone with your child when the baby is asleep.

Page 5 Ellie's story

Ellie doesn't want a new baby in the family. She wants things to stay the same as before.

- Encouraging children to become involved, for example in decorating the baby's room, can help them to feel more positive about the changes a new baby will bring.

Page 9 Liam's story

Liam is worried something bad will happen to his mum when the baby is born.

- Children need reassurance and protection from any worries you might have. Feeling the baby kicking and seeing a scan can help them to understand that all is well.

Page 12 Frankie's story

Frankie doesn't want to have anything to do with the baby. He thinks a tiny baby is boring.

- Even a tiny baby responds to love and attention. Encourage the older sibling to build a relationship with the baby straight away.

Page 15 Mia's story

Mia is jealous of the new baby. She feels left out.

- Extra attention and reassurance that he or she is still very important and loved can help children deal with feeling jealous of a new baby.

Page 18 Jade's story

Jade thinks the new baby is a nuisance and that everyone makes too much fuss over him.

- It helps if you do things with your child that don't include the baby so you have uninterrupted, more grown-up time together.

Page 23 Jesse's story

Jesse is fed up because he is always expected to give way to his baby sister.

- It's important that children know they are being treated fairly. Parents can make sure that a baby doesn't always have its own way at the expense of other children.

Page 26 Kayo's story

Kayo is worried that her stepdad won't love her when he has a baby of his own.

- A child feeling threatened by a new baby needs reassurance of their parent's love for them.

Page 28 Playscript, Bonnie and Grace's story

Children could 'perform' the parts in this simple playscript and then discuss what happened. It's an opportunity to reinforce the point that a new baby can be an exciting time for all the family. Things will have to change but those changes can be positive for everyone. They could also write and perform their own play about a new baby.